CAN YOU JUST BE A MAN

By

Virgil L. Hughes

Table of contents

Introduction……

The Beginning……………………..8

Are You A Man…………………..13

Commit…………………………….21

Husband……………………………26

Table of contents

Just Be My father…………………………………32

Give Me Your Heart………………………………37

Hear My Words……………………………………42

Real Communication Please………………………..47

She Is Not Your Mother……………………………52

Table of Content

You're Going to Wait For This..................56

Responsibility.....................................62

Are You Afraid or Is It Fear…..........................68

The Benefits.......................................73

Closing...77

Introduction

In my last book I left off talking about fathers, so I felt
it would be appropriate if I picked up right there. There are
a lot of men out here who refer to themselves as men, but
don't live up to what the characteristics of what one really
is. So I decided by the inspiration of God, to introduce you
to what not only a man is but, what some of the main

characteristic are that define what a man should be according to the knowledge and wisdom imparted to me from God. And yes I know my approach is not like typical authors, but look at the results of what they have contributed to society. Our jails are still over populated with men, our women are still mistreated, and our kids don't have too many men they can look up to as role models. So instead of giving you some long drawn out theory according to facts based on only certain criteria that some man or woman have formulated, I figured I would simplify it, get straight to the point, and do it in a way that you can understand. No I'm not the perfect man; however, I do know that if I can identify a real man from a fake one, you will appreciate it. So without any more of a drawn out introduction, let me introduce you to a man, from a young man's perspective.

The Beginning

In the beginning God created man. Not only did he create man, but created man in his own image. So what does that actually mean? What that means is, everything that God did in his creative ability, and is still doing to this day, we as men should be doing the same. God gave us power and the ability to cause change in every aspect of life, but we as men as a whole, have dropped the ball. God never intended for men to be of lesser value in any area of life, but He intended for us to bear fruit, multiply, increase, transform, and dominate in every area and in everything we come into contact with. After God spoke the world into existence, and filled it with creatures and vegetation, he followed that up with bringing man into existence. His whole purpose for man was to first commune with him daily, dominate, and control everything the exact way He did things in the creations process. So why do we make it hard for ourselves as men to do exactly as God did? Why do we consider ourselves to be lesser than what God gave us the ability to do?

The reason why we don't operate to our full capabilities as men is because we dropped the ball at the initial step. God never intended for us to have things in life and lose fellowship with him. God is a jealous God and will have no other thing or person before him. Another reason why we don't operate as God endowed us to operate is because we see ourselves as our own gods. Men this is an area that we all have struggled with or are still struggling with. We believe that we in ourselves have the right to make decisions, pick our own path, and go about life any way we choose. But who told you that? I'm pretty sure if you go and review your decisions, you will see God wasn't there in your decision. I mean was the choice you made to start doing something a God inspired idea or a self inspired idea? Let me clue you in to something; you will know if it was God or yourself immediately by simply looking at the results. When God is in it, the process is smooth and effortless, and probably required little or no help from you. However, when the decision was all you and none of God, there is a constant struggle to do it or deal with it, which usually leads to that one thing dominating and controlling every part of your life and time. The craziest part of it all is, when it goes bad you ask God what went wrong. First of all, did you ask Him if He want you to embark on that endeavor? Did you even wait and see what God had to say concerning the issue? Or did you just decide to go and do it because it felt right, and now you are paying the consequences of your own actions? God never intended for you to do anything in life, big or small, and not include him in it.

Then you have this other man, who believes he is successful on his own and takes no time to thank God for it. Who gave you the gift? Who positioned you in life to get there? Or do you believe that you did it alone? This man is only one step away from losing it all because a man who thinks he is something is nothing in the sight of God until he humbles himself before God.

So as I close this chapter out I would like to leave you with something. My father tells me all the time that it's not the amount of times you fall that matters it's, what you do after you get up that counts more than anything. What that means is this, no matter how many times you have fallen or missed it get back up but this time start it on a good not. Your beginnings don't dictate your future, because your beginnings could start today, but it's the foundation you establish your beginnings on that will determine your

future. So realize men that without a beginning that is

founded in God then you have nothing.

Are You A Man

Being a man in today's society can be quite complex, in fact it's almost a second job seeing how you have to have this or have that, in order to even get the attention of a woman. You hear women telling other women that "He isn't a man", or telling that man "He isn't a real man". But what is a real man?

I asked God to define what a man is, and he defined a man as, "A provider, leader, visionary, an example, but more than any of those or anything else he is a mediator between God and his family. So in a sense, some of the things women are saying are correct concerning a man. So let's, get a more clear understanding of what God meant.

Let's start with the most essential which is the mediator. A mediator is the middle man, who is hearing directly from the key source, who is responsible for making sure that everything that was conveyed to him is executed. So let's apply that to God and men. God holds men responsible to hear exactly what his intentions for not only his life, but for his family's life if he has one, and anyone he directs him to. It's important as men you build a pure, without a shadow of doubt, relationship with God for the simple fact that people's lives are in your hands. This is especially important if you have a family. If you died and went to heaven the first thing God is going to talk to you concerning is your family, seeing as you're the mediator of it all.

Now, this leads us to the word visionary. He defined visionary as "Someone who understands the purpose and role of what is going on in his life and those surrounding his life". Being a visionary is important and works hand in hand with being the mediator. As the mediator you are liable for all that you hear, but as the visionary, it's your responsibility to not only know what's going on but make sure all around you know. The bible says "The people perish without a vision." So with that being said let me ask you this, what around you is perishing? Is your family sinking? Are you finances never diminishing? Are you continually losing things or having things taken away from your life? What I mean by that is, does it look like nothing is working right for your family or your life? Is there always some sort of issue or strife occurring in the household? I suggest you check the vision or the visionary because somebody missed the meeting. Or if it's just you, does it seem like everything is working one moment, just to have it taken away? You may want to consider going back to your prayer closet and asking God to show you all over again what His vision is for your life.

Secondly you must be a leader as a man. I asked God to define this as well and he said, "A leader is someone who is walking out his course that was given to him, and is executing it in an infallible way". Well in order to do it the way God intended it you had to hear it exactly as he told you. This is why hearing from God is essential to your own life. You don't want to be a man who is trying to lead, but doesn't understand where you are going, and ends up going in circles while accomplishing nothing in the process except kicking up dust. Who wants to follow a man who can't lead effectively? He has no direction, no sense of urgency, and is relying on his own intuition to help lead. If I were someone who was following this man, I would ask him to lay the vision out so I can see the route we were taking, just to make sure he knew what he was talking about. And if he doesn't, I would advise you to make your

own detour and find out where you're suppose to be going.

Next, to be a man you must lead by example. This is

going to be a very interesting one here so bear with me. So

what is the definition of example? God said, "To be an

example is, to do only those things that reflect integrity". In

other words I should only do those things in front of you

that I want instilled in you. I should be aware of what I'm

doing in front of you and away of you because failure is not

an option. My father says all the time, "I won't do anything

in front of you or away from you that isn't going to reflect

my heart". That's an awesome statement. But why don't we

see more men acting like this, or demonstrating this in

relationships with their wives, children, families, church, or

work environment? The main reason why most men are not

leading by example is due to the belief in themselves that I

can keep this hidden and no one will know. Well, sorry to

burst your bubble sir but, in this era of technology it is nearly impossible to do something and not get caught. Plus, whatever is done in the dark or secret places, or so they seem secret, will be shown. Have you not seen all the things that have been brought out into the open? We are in a time where God is not going to be mocked, and as a man you should want to be a righteous man standing at the forefront saying, "I ran my course, and was an example to all men". If you're going to do something sir, and no I'm not condoning anything, but don't be a coward and hide it. Be a man and do it openly.

Finally we have the word "provider". God defined provider as "Someone who takes on the sole responsibility of all matters concerning those involved. How can you call you yourself a man and you don't work? A Man that doesn't work doesn't eat nor can he provide for himself or those included in his life. What disturbs me the most concerning all of this is, you have some women who are ok with a man with no stability concerning his finances. Granted that number is probably a lot smaller than I imagine, but they are out there. But that's just a woman who is desperate for a man. A man will keep a job or do legal things to be able to continue to provide for himself and for his family. If I was a woman, I wouldn't want a man who couldn't provide. But if I were a woman with kids, he couldn't come ten feet of me. Men this is an unattractive characteristic, and you just need to stop making excuses for being lazy. God gives every man a talent and gift, you just need to get up, talk to Him, and let him lead you in the way to go. It's just that simple.

So in a nut shell, we see God never intended for man to not be like him, but he intended for him to exemplify him in the areas of being a mediator, visionary, leader, example, and a provider. But if you don't talk to God and get the first part straight by hearing him (and by hearing I mean clearly) then you will always live a hit and miss lifestyle. So do us all a favor and devote time for him, He has a lot he wants to say if you will just listen.

Commit

This subject matter is one of those areas that most men struggle with for a majority of their lives. And it's not that they don't make it obvious that it they are not looking for one, in fact they let it be known from the beginning. But, why are men afraid of committing?

The first reason why men are scared of committing is due to a fear of losing out on something. And when I say losing out on something, that's not me implying someone better than the woman they are interested in or dating, but out on the fun. And when I say fun, I mean the flirting, the attention, and the opportunities presented to them from various women. No man will tell you the truth, but we thrive on this at points in our lives, especially, if we are still discovering the level of women we can attract. See what is going through this man's mind is this: she is trying to trap me and I'm too young to be tied down to just one woman in their life. What you have to understand about this man at this point in his life is that they are more prone to cheat in a relationship, even if they are in a good relationship. Your probably wondering what can I say to justify my statement and that's simple, after so much attention from someone, one or two things will occur: he will either do it and hope he doesn't get caught up, or he will allow it to settle in his mind to the degree of he's already committed the act, so it will eventually occur if the opportunity presents itself. Women avoid this man until he gets this out of his system, which could be at an early age in life or in a later point in their life.

The next reason why men avoid commitment is due them feeling as though they don't have enough to offer you in order to be with him. It's not that he doesn't want to be with you, it's just his fear of not being able to keep you if someone else comes along. You see, what goes through a man at this moment is simple, he doesn't want to go all in then lose you when someone else comes along that has it. And yes I know you might be saying "Why are you trying to be with her you're not fully capable of giving her all that she needs"? To be honest no person will be fully capable of giving you exactly what you need when they first meet. However, if you're basing this off of monetary fulfillment only, then she doesn't need to be with him in the first place. But men, let me say this to you. I have been in a situation where I thought that if I didn't have certain things then I couldn't be there for her like she needed. You know what though, I was terribly wrong. First of all realize like I said earlier, you won't have everything she needs when you meet her so don't act like you will. Secondly, if you do lose everything, don't run from her, but you don't stay in that situation long either. What I mean by this is simple: don't lose something, get comfortable with not having something, and becomes a burden to her. She doesn't deserve that, but you also shouldn't run either. If she extends her help to you, then understand she believes in you, and that takes a lot for women to do.

The last reason why men avoid commitment is this: He never wanted to commit in the first place. I know it sounds simple but, you have so many women who believe they can change the mind of a man. I probably should have said this one first but I couldn't for one reason, women just don't get it. This was for men but it applies for women as well. If a man says he doesn't want to be in a relationship then don't try to force him into being in one. Nine times out of ten, if a man says "Not now" then take it as not now. But you know what, you still have some women who believe that they can change his mind, and then you blame the man for not wanting to be committed, but you can't. He told you from jump where he was concerning a relationship, but you took it upon yourself to not listen. So he isn't at fault, none what so ever. So before you decide to cast blame for him not wanting to be committed, evaluate the situation.

Husband

There are so many men out there that are married but continue to live the single life. Here's my question to you married men: If you knew you weren't ready for that commitment then why did you get married? Here's my next question to you married men: Why do you still affiliate yourself with single individuals knowing that you're only setting yourself up for failure? Okay, and here's another question for you married men: Why doesn't anyone know you're married nor have they met your wife? All of these questions that I have asked, I will answer! In fact, with my responses to these questions I may answer more of your concerns, so let us begin.

Tell me why do men get married to their spouses, but knew deep inside he wasn't ready, pretend like it's all good and have no issues or concerns before the wedding, come back after the honeymoon, and continue to live the single life.? I will tell you what the problem is! The only reason or possible reasons he got married were due to him feeling like it was his time, or someone pushed him into, or the woman pressured him into. Men, who get married because they have reached a certain level in life or age, are setting themselves up for failure. First of all, this man doesn't realize the significance of what marriage is and has taken the liberty of putting it into a goal or mission in life category. He also has taken all the responsibility of what only God can control, and has determined himself to be right for marriage. However, all he is doing is setting himself up for divorce. People like this rush into in and end up rushing out of it because they really didn't even know the person they decided they were going to marry. And you know who pays for it more than anything? The woman does! In her mind she believes he is marrying her out of love when in all actuality, he's only marrying her based on time. Why do this to any woman, especially if she is a great woman? Don't be foolish man, and do something that is only a status symbol or a life achievement because you're not going to hurt yourself more than you're going to hurt her. Be a man and just wait until God tells you it's time, or shows you who she is. And when he shows you who she is, it doesn't necessarily mean it's time to jump on her. He might be showing you her as a motivation to get yourself together for her.

Next if you're a married man, why are you still socializing yourself with single individuals or placing yourself where single people gather? You know what upsets me more than anything? Seeing a man, who's married, out and about with single woman and men, or at a gathering and your wife isn't anywhere to be found. How disrespectful of a man are you? You have to be foolish or something, because you being there is the ultimate set up. First of all let me start here. When you get married "man", you give up all of the single life and become unified with your spouse. So why is she not with you? Let me clue you in, he hasn't officially accepted it in his mind just yet. He still believes that it's ok to get up with the guy's and run the streets. The only thing that is going to occur is you cheating. I remember hearing my father say, "What do a married man and a single man have in common, outside of being friends"? He would follow that up with "Nothing". And it's a true statement; they have nothing in common anymore. A married mans mindset is suppose to be family oriented and future driven concerning him and his spouse. A single man is still searching for his spouse. What usually occurs here is this: the married man either rubs off on the single man or, the single man rubs off on the married man. There is no other way of it occurring. And for you women who allow your husband's to spend all that time in those situations, don't get mad if he does do something, because he is really only doing what your ok with. When that man leaves, my suggestion is you go with him. Let it be known who you are, which is leading me in the final point in this chapter.

The only reason why he doesn't want to take you with him to places is for these two reasons: he has someone who he is entertaining, or he doesn't want to limit what he could possibly have by allowing it to be known he is married. See these are the men that really irritate me. Co-workers don't know he is married, boss doesn't know he is married, and friends don't know he is married either. In fact, the only people who know he is married are you, both of your families, and those who were at the wedding. And I know

your probably wondering what evidence I have to prove it?

This man probably takes his ring off, comes home with it

not on, or leaves it at home and says it was a mistake.

That's like me saying I forgot to put on under garments.

Men don't forget to do things like that unless he had

intentions of doing so. So women if your husband is doing

this, you may want to check him now before he checks out

later.

Just Be My Father

The hardest thing in this day and age is for a father to be a father, and not be the best friend. So many times I see fathers trying to relate to their children on the level of a friend. God never intended for you to have that sort of relationship with your children, in fact, I believe this is the biggest mistake parents make. What usually occurs in this relationship is one of two things: the child grows up not understanding the role they should play as the child and have not sense of respect for authority or, the parent takes on full responsibility for the child's actions, but never does anything to correct them.

The whole purpose of God blessing you with a child is for you to instill in them the core values of God, lead them to where their suppose to go in life, and help them to establish themselves knowing, they will succeed in all they do as long as God is the focal of it all. But how can you do that as a friend father? You can't in fact it will be nearly impossible. First of all, a friend will be there for good times and sometimes for the bad. So is that the role you want to play as a father? I myself as a father can't have, nor do I want this relationship because this type usually ends in a bad way. Growing up I never understood why my father made sure that we had more moments of serious communication, then those of laughter, or him taking me somewhere to buy me things. As I grew older, and saw how our relationship evolved, it made more sense on so many more levels. The first thing it did was instill in me respect for him. This generation both now and the upcoming have a large displacement of respect for people who are older than they are, but they also have no respect for themselves. My father made sure that if I was around anyone of a significant age difference that I referred to them as sir or ma 'am. No matter the circumstances I had to show them the respect, and if I didn't, he was close by listening and would correct me immediately. These men who want to be friends with their children don't even want to be acknowledged as the father, especially if they have a young countenance. All that you are doing is making a fool of yourself by trying to hold on to something you lost many years ago.

The other thing with this friend relationship between a child and the father is it slows down the development of the child. How can you tell your child to grow up when they see you clowning around with them like you're their age? Where is the guidance? Where is the example? There isn't one, so the child is forced to learn on their own, even though you are there as the parent. Just to be honest they really don't want to ask you anything, or talk to you about anything because they see the lack of maturity exuberating from you. Children can sense just like adults, that you are not the one they need to run to for guidance, which is why befriending you child is not the answer.

More importantly then anything is the relationship the child see's you having with God. My father prayed every day, the same time, and same place. He made sure we heard him every day, as a matter of fact he made sure he would takes us in with him to pray just to let be known he serves God. What occurred from this is more amazing then anything. My level of respect for him grew, my ability to confide in him grew, and my trust grew in him. He never once in my life tried to come at me as a friend, because the father is the only friend a child needs. A child is more prone to open up to the person or persons who are correcting, directing, assisting, and listening to what they are saying then someone who is attempting to understand them as a friend.

So please, know and understand that being a father is the best and only friend your child deserves and needs to become the best person that they can be in life.

Give Me Your Heart

The heart of a man is one of the most delicate things in life. To be quite honest with you, it's the only thing of true value we have in our lives, outside of salvation. This could explain why when give it our all, we are all in, and if it's broken then it takes forever to heal. There are only a few reasons why men are so hesitant to give their heart to someone yet they each are so true. The reasons are, it's been broken before, never actually went all in with his heart before, or it still hasn't healed from the previous time. And unlike women, men have the ability to hide it as if it's ok until it reveals it's self on its own.

The greatest fear for any man is to have his heart broken. What women have to under is that it takes a lot for a man to go all in with his heart. Once a man goes all in with his heart, his emotions comes with it and his life is in the palm of your hands. But for someone who has never experienced a man whose heart is broken let me give you the symptoms. He rarely gets emotional with you or concerning you, he always is comparing you to his ex (which happens to be the person who broke it), and he is looking for no commitment from you. The reason he acts this way is simple, he is still holding on to a prayer that there is a possibility things will change for him and her. Again no man wants the broken heart, and the only thing that can heal his heart is the person who broke it and time.

Now for most women this is just a refresher, but to some this is going to be breaking news. Most men have never, and I mean never, given their all, which is their heart. Most don't know how to, while others refuse to, but it's a part of maturing into a man. With the way television,

music, billboards, and all other ways they influence society
with, they almost make it illegal for a man to be with one
woman, yet alone give her your heart. Let's think about
something for a minute. Why in the world would a man
give his heart to just one woman, when you have so many
women out there just waiting on someone to make a move
on them? Plus at the rate that we all are going, women
won't need a man to much more anyway, but that's a
different subject matter. All I have to say concerning this
one is simple, if women would mandate that men went all
in with them or nothing at all, life would be a lot easier for
everyone.

Finally we have the unhealed heart of a man. Women
let me say this, beware this man because he is on a mission,
but I will talk about that in just one minute. Men, it's
neither right nor fair to a woman to deal with your unhealed
heart. See what most men go and do in this situation is act

out sexually, to try and block it mentally. But guess what, it doesn't work. For you information sir, all that will show you is that your heart isn't there. As a matter of fact it will make it worse for yourself if you allow yourself to go through with it. So why don't you do save yourself the stress and save the woman the drama and the pain of dealing with it by just allowing yourself time to heal. It will be work it in the end.

So with all that has been said I will leave with this. Men, consider the state your heart and emotions are in before dealing with a woman. She could be all that you need or all that you wish you never met just don't get confused because you're in a vulnerable place. To my women, don't impose yourself on a man or force him to give you his heart and you not know if he has had it broken, never given it all before, or is still healing. Not knowing can be detrimental to your own heart and emotions. The heart is a paradox in itself and needs no more assistance in

making it more misunderstood from us adding our own

issues to it.

Hear My Words

As a man, you need to realize that the only thing you have that's of any value to any woman is your word. They may not admit it, but your money, cars, houses and anything else that falls into the materialistic category is only icing on the relationship. Think about it for a second, what frustrates your woman more than anything? What frustrates any woman for that matter when it comes to men? Lies! Women will work with any man they love or are interested in, no matter the issue except for lying. And the women that decide to deal with a man's lies are only dealing with him for only a few reasons: she hasn't been truly hurt by his lies, he hasn't been caught yet, or she's doing her dirt too, so overlooking his lies will cover up her

lies as well.

    Men, your words are all you have with anyone, but

especially with your woman. She will stick with you

through it all if you just keep your word. You could be on

the verge of losing it all but she will stay because you never

hurt her with deception. However, here's my question to

the men, why can't you be transparent with the person you

chose to be in a relationship with? The most embracing

thing you can do is allow yourself to allow nothing but the

truth, good or bad, to flow out of you towards her. She will

love you more, and trust you more, and confide in you

more, when she knows nothing but the truth comes out of

you. She also knows that if you make a mistake, you will

let her know instead of hiding it, and finding out on her on.

Nothing disappoints a woman more than being the last

person to find out that you have done something. Nothing disappoints anyone more than finding out something last when the person has been there all the time. And what makes it worse it that you come with the horrible excuse of "I didn't know how to tell you" or "I didn't want to hurt you". Please your intentions from the beginning were to deceive, if they weren't then why hide it? Like my father always says "If you love someone you will be honest, no exceptions." And yes we all know the truth hurts, but lies hurt worse, so refrain from doing so.

For you men who think you won't get caught, I have a news flash, you always get caught. There are only two ways to get caught men and that's either by you telling on yourself or you doing something you usually don't do. Men, let's be honest for a second. Do you think that you are that gifted that you cannot be caught? This is the first mistake men make right here ladies, thinking he won't get caught! We believe that no matter what we do we are invincible especially if we have been getting away with it for some time. The only reason why you haven't be caught is she is waiting to see how long you're going to attempt to play her for the fool. Women pick up on the little stuff men. They know when something is wrong because they pay attention. They listen to you more than you realize. If you think I'm telling a story, the next time you get in an argument with her, listen to all the exact details she tells you concerning the issues she's addressing with you. They know when you're lying. They know when you're telling the truth. They know when you've been distracted and they know when you make detours. They know you better than you think they do. And you know the ultimate way to see if he is lying, check the phone, emails or any other means of communication. This is the number one way to know. If he

is hiding all of it from you then you need to worry, and I
will leave it at that

Now, let's discuss the last reason why you're not
getting caught: she doesn't care because she is doing her
own thing. Don't be foolish men because she isn't. Women
will only do what they see you do or feel you're doing, so if
they feel your lying then they will run will it and lie to.
Once a woman is lied to and moves on emotionally and
mentally, you might as well keep going. Sorry but it's over
men and there is no turning back

Real Communication Please

In today's society, communication is so vital on so many levels, yet in the one area it's needed the most we have allowed that area to dwindle away. As a matter of fact, we all have fallen victim to this at various points in our lives, but we have done nothing to rectify the issue. We have video chat, texting, email, and other various means of communication, but what happen to personal one on one communication? However, do you know who the only person benefiting from this, but at the same time suffering? It's our men. They are suffering all around with even knowing what to say to a woman, yet alone court one the proper way. What happen to sitting down, looking that person in the eyes, and match a voice to what's being expressed instead of having to guess what emotion is being conveyed? No one wants to put in the effort anymore like they use to. We all are too busy about nothing of true meaning and value. You know what all of this new age technology did for everyone? It made it easy for you to be emotionally detached from the person you're conversing with. I myself have fell victim to this several times, just to be brought back to reality by someone who wants to hear my voice. This also made it easier for you not to use integrity. But you say "How is that possible"? Well I'm glad you asked because you're about to get all the answers you need.

You know why men love this new era of technology? They love it because it allows them the ability to not focus all of their attention on one person, convey non-emotional feelings that appear to demonstrate they care, it just makes it easier to operate in deception. Men, let me set the record

straight here for one moment. Even though we love to think
we have this supernatural ability to focus and multitask
when it comes to women, we really don't. One real woman
is more than enough for you if she is truly a woman in all
aspects, so you trying to remember more than one is going
to be nearly impossible. However, you have these digital
woman or "digital hoes" as a few of my associates and I
refer to them as, which make it easy. They pretty much
know there role and stick with it, so you not devoting all of
your attention to them isn't nothing new. See with them a
simple "hey" or "how are you" through text is enough, but
a woman will make you call. See women put pressure on
men to step out of the normal routine, but you have these
other women who try it but eventually bend and continue to
allow this, which is not acceptable. So how do you fix this
is ladies? Here are a few easy steps: when he text you,
reply back with "call me". If he continues on, then don't

respond until he does. What eventually happens is he will grow tired of the no response and become frustrated by it. And finally just ignore him completely and when he calls tell him this is the only way he will hear from him if it's after work. The only time texting or emailing should be permitted is while you're working, otherwise, men pick up the phone and use it

The next reason why men have no problem with the various forms of communication it taking the actual dating or courting process out of it, so you really aren't getting pure interaction with them. For those of you who don't know what courting is, let me explain. Courting is an old school term they used, that let it be known you were seeing this one person. Courting is one on one time, looking in the eyes of that woman and feeling her soul, understanding her emotions, and just embracing her at that moment. Nothing demonstrates true interest then sitting down, talking, looking that person in the eyes, and listening. This is also intimacy. In fact this should be considered of a higher form of intimacy for the simple fact she is allowing you in mentally where everything about her is. The reason men avoid this is for one reason: it leaves an open door policy. What woman do you know wants a text buddy/relationship with someone she is interested in, but can't get alone time with him. To get the results you want, mandate he has at least one date night, every week, at the same time. And don't waiver from it either; because the minute you do you're giving signs of condoning his behavior. Just don't do it

She Is Not Your Mother

Have you ever met a boy, who believes his mother is the ultimate when it comes to the example of what it is to be a woman? Yes I referred to him as a boy, for the simple fact he is not behaving like a man. What man in his right mind wants a woman exactly like his mother? Yes he should want some attributes or characteristics of who she is, but to compare every aspect of who she is with the person you're seeing is pointless. The reasons why men look for women like their mothers are for simple reasons: she made him feel like he is the only one that mattered, she was simple and perceived things the way he wanted to, or she could just be the opposite and be an overall great woman which still doesn't justify his actions. So let's get into this.

The first reason why men look for a woman like his mother is because she put him first. Granted that is a great trait, however this also can cause unnecessary issues. Most men, who have mothers of this type, also have issues with not being the main priority. You see these men have never been second and will have problems dealing with not being first. For example, say you always compromise with him over almost every issue that occurs, but this time you decide not to. Trust me when I say this, his reaction is going to be that of a child. Most men like this also have a problem with not getting what they want, so look out for the issues that are about to arise from this. See he was told no, but she would break, and in the end would give in to what he wanted, so why should you be allowed to tell him no. Advice to the women who deal with this man: Let him go!

Then you have the man child, who was raised by a simple woman, who made her son a god. And no I'm not coming down on mothers who do so, but look at the overall picture and the results of doing so. Most men come from single households, where the mother ordains the child the man of the house, seeing how men can't be responsible fathers. Most men like this have a problem with authority, since even at an early age he had the final say. However, these men who are made gods have problems with authority and end up in two places: dead or jail. Even the thought of being denied something, throws them in to an uproar. Again I say run because these are also the abusive type of men who handle it only one way and that's by force.

Finally you have the mother who was in fact the perfect idea of what a mother is, but guess what this does to your boy? It means he will look for perfection and never find it which means he will be a heart breaker. In other words he will involve himself with various women, who in fact could be great women for his life, but let them be missing one thing and it's over. She could comb her hair a certain way or do things opposite of what he saw his mother do and he isn't going to be there, believe that. You see his one issue is his perfect mother and will never acknowledge her as being the problem. My answer to this as well is run, because there is no telling how long it will take before he realizes that she may be perfect as far as a parent is concerned but when it comes to his life, she shouldn't be the determining factor.

You're Going To Wait For This...

You know it pisses me of sometimes to hear people saying you should wait months or a certain time before embarking on something sexual with your partner. Who are you to first, tell someone how long they should wait before having sex? Then, what you are telling them is totally backwards, and shouldn't be said in the first place! IF you're going to give advice, then why don't you say what needs to be said instead of saying what your readers want to read. And if you think this is directed to you specifically, it probably is, so let's get into this.

Who are you to tell someone how long they should wait before having sex? Sex is something that shouldn't be played with and shouldn't have a time limit on when it should occur. All your really saying is that it's okay to have sex, just give it time to be justified. Well let me correct what should have been stated. There is no time limit to when you should have sex; in fact you should wait until you're his wife bottom line! No we are not perfect and we all make mistakes in the process sometimes, but don't continue to bump your head on the same mistake. Men and women both know that once you have sex things change. Women develop a deeper feeling and men either stay or they leave. That's what happens when you put a time limit on it. So why do it? The reason why we do it is because of fear. Fear of losing something you probably never had in the first place. Fear that if you don't give him what he wants he will leave you for another. Listen it all boils down to this, if this man really wants you trust me he will wait. If you already had sex and you want to it right and not have sex, again he will wait. If he doesn't then he never wanted you from the beginning. Now that's the truth.

Secondly, the right way of doing this is to do it the way the bible said it's suppose to be done. You meet the woman God has for you. You court or get to know this woman. You bring it before the Lord, because you're going to honor God in this marriage. Then you get married and have all the sex you want. SO then why isn't it going this way? The reason why it's not going in that order is this. First you have a sexually driven society that is propagating that sex is ok in every area of life. Think about it for a minute. Sex is on the television, on the radio, in the schools, and yes in our churches. And the reason why it's like this is because; some crazy individual is scared to lose money, instead of doing the right thing. Well let me speak for you. Having sex with someone doesn't solidify your relationship if anything it makes it more unstable. Sex doesn't make you a man or a woman at an early age; it robs you of your life and your innocence. And sex to be honest with you is nothing if it's not with someone who loves you for you and not how you feel. All of what I just said goes for men, women, boys, and girls. Everyone seems to be missing this point in life of knowing what comes from having sex. Don't be foolish and end up doing something you will regret or get something you're not prepared for. But you know what's even crazier than anything I've said thus far? You have men and women who have become victims of sexual abuse on the giving end and on the receiving end, but won't say anything to fix what's going on, but will sit back in a judgmental mindset and talk down about it. IF you're not going to help fix it then don't add your two cents to it.

Finally let me direct this to the men. Sex is not for your amusement, sensual stimulation, to get another notch under your belt. Sex is an intimate act that she is demonstrating her love for you and you just want to let something off? And you wonder why women act up the way they do when you just up and go. So many words I want to use, but I have to maintain my manners right now. Your penis doesn't have a mind of its own, it's just you don't have enough self control to tell it no. Then let's say you do love the woman your with after you have sex, but she doesn't want to do it like that anymore. Your ignorant self can't handle it and still leaves. All because she doesn't want to ruin something she believes is the right thing for her life. See you need to see beyond your own stupidity and think for one second of someone other than yourself. Plus sex cannot be that important to the point of you not being able to control it. See what you really are, is a weak minded, sensually driven man, who believes that sex is what comes with being with you. But again like I said earlier you're not at total fault for your actions, but you're also not going to use society as your escape route either. Man up and just say enough is

enough, and do it right.

Responsibility

With the title of being a man, come the responsibilities of life that I don't believe all the self proclaimed men are aware of. You know the ones who talk the talk that a man really would talk, but don't walk the walk of a real man. You know what personifies the word "swagger" to me? A man who doesn't pretend he's somewhere he's not, but see's where he is going and goes for it. A man that grabs life with both hands and doesn't settle for what he's been given. So be prepared to get your feeling hurt if you don't fit the role or the man your with is a great illusionist.

The responsibilities of a real man never end in fact, they are an ongoing, ever evolving process, but his first responsibility is himself. Men when you look in the mirror what do you see? Do you see someone successful or someone who is just now realizing who he is? The first thing you need to do is figure out your purpose in life. God has given you a creative ability, purpose and plan in life, which will affect not only, you but all of those who you surround yourself with. So what is your reason for being here? Let me assist you. What is it in life that you're good at doing? That might be the area that your will have success with. Or what is it that you have a major issue or concern with and could see yourself helping people with that require little or hardly any effort on your part? That is another helpful idea as to what you are here for. Now take that and apply that to life and I bet you will be successful at what you do.

As a man your next responsibility is to be a father and provider for your family. You know I am totally disgusted by men who want to be with a woman who has kids but, doesn't want to be fully responsible for them. These men for the lack of words, are quick to say they are not his kids so why should I do something for them? And will follow it up with "Tell them to call and ask their daddy". Buddy you really fell off of a cliff and burst your head wide open. That's not logical or rational in any aspect. And if that is the case, then respond back by saying then you aren't the one, and politely direct him to the nearest exit. Women mandate it be an all or nothing exclusive package and if he's not willing to operate like that then don't step to the plate pretending to be.

Furthermore, let's get something straight once and for all; a father doesn't have to be the biological father in order to be considered the father. As a man I would marry a woman with kids, love her kids probably more then she would expect and want nothing to do with or from the father. But before you take the responsibilities of this role realize this: there is no backing out of it, so don't decide to leave later on because it will affect the child or children to see the man that represents their father leave. Secondly make sure your financially stable enough or planning to be able to provide for that situation. You may have a woman who says you're not responsible for them, but let's be serious. You would be a fool to not step in all the way with that and assist, but she would be even more foolish to not make you. You wanted her and what came with it, so hand it all over and bring it together. No separate anything, and if it is both should have access to it all.

And finally, to the men who have kids but are not financially supporting your kids; you are the most irresponsible individual I have ever seen in my life. The fact that you're living your life knowing you have responsibilities to provide for your children, but you see fit that you live your life instead. Do us all a favor and don't call yourself a man. How dare you to not provide for your kids. I don't care if it's legal or not, you should be somewhere exhausting every effort possible to see that you have funds available to your kids. You think it's fair to her to have to kick out all her money to make sure they have the things they need? She didn't make them by herself, well in some cases she did, then you should contribute. The name father comes with a price tag so if you're not prepare to be one then don't go sticking your penis in everything you see fit to place it in. But let me also say this to the women who have a man who is providing for his kids, your kids are not there to supply a continual cash flow for you amusement, nor are they to be used as some sort of ransom. All you will do is push a man who is trying to be the best father he can be away, because all you see is dollar signs. Money is important but it is also not the final say in the situation.

So to my men be responsible and do the things you know your suppose to be doing a man, otherwise don't call yourself anything that factors in remotely close to being associated with the word man, father, dad, provider, etc., etc.

Is it Fear or Are You Afraid?

Life has a way of convincing men to fear life instead of being afraid of it. And I know some of you would say he shouldn't do either, but let's be honest for a moment. There will come a point in life where he only has two choices; he will fear life or he will be afraid. Yes I know some would argue that the two are the same but, I'm here to let you know that they are not. Let's begin.

What is fear? I asked God to define fear and he said. "Fear is a tormenting mental state of mind that leads them into believing they can't overcome various circumstances and situations". He went further do state that fear is "destructive". So with that being said, why in the world would a man allow fear to dwell with him, yet along let the word fear come out of his mouth? Fear coming out of the

mouth of a man is irresponsible. Yes life has its up and

downs, but when you believe you can't go on any further

then you're no more good to yourself or anyone else. I can

hear my father saying "Fear brings torment", and that's a

very true statement. Have you ever seen a man who is

fearful of what life will do to him? He sits around and waits

for it to happen, becomes mentally unstable, and stagnant.

Everything that proceeds out of his mouth reflects fear.

From spending money to going to the store, he fears the

end. But you know why it's like this? Simple, he has no

trust in himself but more importantly then anything he has

no trust whatsoever in God. How do I know this? I was that

man at one point in my life. And being fearful caused me to

make decisions in life I wouldn't usually make, which put

me in compromising situations. I'm my only fear. And

what that means is that if I fear what I'm going to do then I am no longer any good to anyone else. The way that you rectify this and move out of fear is to operate in faith. You have to trust God with your life. That's the first and most important step of them all. Faith is the opposite of fear, just like light is the opposite of darkness. Secondly, speak words that resemble faith only and not fear. The tongue is just like the pen of the ready writer. You speak failure you get failure. You speak faith you get results. It's just that easy.

I also asked God to define what the word afraid meant and he said, "To be unclear and uncertain concerning something, but you see your way through it. He also said "Being afraid can be compared to foggy vision. You know you're going in the right direction but you don't see further then what's in front of you". He went further to state this, "We as believers, especially men, have a harder time seeing beyond our own capabilities, which is the fog. However if the fog would clear out long enough to allow you to see, then you would realize that: God and his angels have been there all along; what you have been asking for is right in your grasp; and no one said it would be handed to you with no effort involved. What you have to understand about being afraid is this; you know and understand that in a moment's notice you, can and will be fine. But you also need to understand that you must operate in faith, and be confident. My advice to you concerning being afraid get your mouth and your actions to line up with the word of God, and all will be fine….trust me.

So men, know and understand this; you decide your fates in life when an attack comes against you. Will you fear life or be afraid of what's going to occur next? Will you stop because there is no visibility and exercise your faith? Or will you crumble and return to the earth where men were formed from? Because if fear has gripped your life and you don't do anything about it you might as well

just leave here because you're no more earthly good.

The Benefits

Now that we have identified some of the key
components of being a man, as well as understanding how
to identify someone is pretending to be a man, what are the
benefits of being a man? Well as a man, there are many
benefits to look forward to. There are many benefits from
God, from society, and in your personal life that you obtain
once you reach the level of being a man.

The first benefit of being a man is having a relationship
with God. Yes I know it doesn't sound like much to some
but to me, this is the best benefit of them all. You have to
understand something, having God in your life as a man is
a phenomenal relationship that cannot be compared to any
other. When you have God on your side as a man, you are

the top of the line type of man. Knowing you have access to the main source of everything you need is a great feeling. Just knowing that you don't have to play the hit or miss game with life is amazing in itself. Realizing that your life is in his hands and you don't have to force anything to occur is another great benefit. Divine health, continuous prosperity, salvation, and the list could go on and on for miles. Those are the benefits of being a man of god, so why would you not want to accept them.

The next benefits that a man gains from being a real man are from society. When people realize that you're an honest hard working man, they actually respect you more, value you your opinion, and rely on you as an example to other. But with me saying that, let me say this; Society is a visually driven system that requires you to look a certain way in order to be respected. No I'm not saying you have to lose your own style, but you may have to make some changes. If you haven't realized certain levels of business have certain attire they wear on a regular basis. For example corporate america, they all wear some form of black or navy blue suit, with the sky blue shirt under it, and the oxford shoes, and a tie. So why in the world would they respect you if your clothes are falling off of you or you look like you bought them two sizes too small? They won't. But let's get back to where we were. Society has a way of categorizing you based on appearance and when they see you fit their standards or surpass them, they welcome you with open arms. The respect they give is beneficial to you. So instead of trying to be an individual all the time, allow yourself the opportunity to reap the rewards of what society has to offer instead of reaping only what they are forced to give you, which isn't much.

Finally the rewards you receive in your own personal life. There is nothing more satisfying as a man then reflecting on all the things you were able to accomplish. Knowing that you are a success in all areas of your life deserves a round of applause if you're doing great things. And if you're doing it on the magnitude where your now an example for others and can help them to reach their maximum potential is even greater. Then knowing as a parent of a child and they are great kids and respect you for being a man in their life is the top layer of the cake. But then having your woman, your wife, right there just smiling and applauding you, and esteeming you because she sees your hard work paying off is a priceless feeling.

I know I didn't, get into details like I probably could have, but you understand what I'm conveying. And if you don't here is what I'm saying. The benefits of being a God fearing and loving, motivated man, with a found vision and purpose in life has its benefits, you just have to go get them.

Closing

As I close out this book, I asked God what he wanted me to leave you with. He said "Integrity". As men we are responsible to not only ourselves but to all those who we encounter on a daily basis. When we as men do not operate to our full potential, we are letting those who are looking up to us down. We are their examples, but if we cannot be examples to ourselves, then what good are we to anyone? Our women need us to step up and impart wisdom, knowledge, discipline, and respect for everyone into this generation, but it starts with us. Take the focus off of how much you can obtain in life and look around you , and you will see just how much we are need to make a lasting effect on our society. It's time to step it up in our relationships with God, it's time we step up our relationships with our women, and it's time we step up our relationships with our children. The jails are over populated and it seems as though living for nothing and dying is the goal now. Its time out for the games we have played long enough, and it's time to take back our communities as well as society. Fulfill your dreams men, it's never too late to start, and if you're a father, leave something for your children to remember you by in a good way. Love God with all of your heart and he will direct your path.

Thank You

I first have to give the entire honor to God for giving
me an ear to hear and a gift of understanding, to impart the
knowledge I have thus far. Without him none of who I am
or who I am becoming would be possible. For that I am
forever grateful. Don't ever give up on your dreams
because you don't know when or where God will use you.

To my father Carl R. Turner Sr., I am so thankful for
having you as an example of who a God fearing man of
God is. I know that growing up I wasn't the easiest child to
have, but you never gave up on me nor did you release your
hand off of my life. You believed in me when I gave up on
myself. I felt your prayers, your concern, but more
importantly your love for me, many miles away and I just

want to thank you. I know I failed you many times but thank you for never judging me or quitting on me. Thank you for instilling in me all the things you have. I didn't know I had so much of you locked up in the inside of me until I started writing and now I hear you more clearly now then I have ever in my life. And I thank you with all my heart.

To you my family, friends, love ones, and church family. Thank you for being there for me. Thank you for your love. Thank you for just being real.

To you…and you know who you are, I owe you so much right now for the way you have affected my life. The only way I know how to really word this is by putting it in my book for it to be expressed everywhere. You complete me and I think of you on every hour of every day, of every week. And when we are not around or I don't hear you I feel incomplete. To some this may sound crazy but to you, this is just me reaffirming what I said because I meant

every word of it. What the future holds I don't know but

whatever it has in store I'm ready to embrace it.

To you my readers thank you for your support.

www.ingramcontent.com/pod-product-compliance
Lightning Source LLC
Chambersburg PA
CBHW021233280526
45784CB00005B/2090